The
Sacred Purpose

*How Youth Sports Organizations Can
Do More to Prepare Athletes for Life*

Dennis E. Coates, Ph.D.

Printed in the United States of America
 First Summit Publishing
 P.O. Box 1655
 Newport News, VA 23601
 757-873-3700

Cover design and interior composition:
Paula Schlauch

ISBN: 978-0-9850156-6-4

I've been working in adult learning for nearly 40 years, delivering training programs and assessment and development technologies to millions of employees worldwide. All these solutions were the product of my passionate interest in the human brain and how it learns and creates behavior patterns.

About five years ago, I had an important insight: **The ineffective behaviors I was helping adults change were habits that had been reinforced for decades.**

This realization accounted for the challenges they faced when trying to improve skills at this stage in life. The insight also caused me to ask this question: **Why didn't these adults learn effective ways of dealing with each other in the first place, when they were young?**

The answer, of course, is that this kind of training has never been a part of a school curriculum. People learn how to communicate and deal with life's challenges in a random, unstructured way—"on the street," so to speak. The results are quite diverse.

Thinking realistically about this issue led me to create the kinds of learning technologies that produce lasting changes in behavior. It also caused me to recognize an opportunity: **To help youth work on effective communication skills and personal strengths—before they enter the workplace.**

What could be more important than this? Parents want the best for their kids; they hope and plan for their brightest future. Communities support programs to prepare young people for life and to deal with less fortunate "at-risk" children.

Consequently, achieving this "sacred purpose" has become a big part of my work. In addition to bringing brain-based learning systems to adults, we now offer similar systems for achievement-oriented teenagers and the adults who mentor them.

These systems are intended to complement—not replace—the activities that have always had an enormous influence on youth. In my own life, I owe a great deal to my years in the Boy Scouts and my participation in sports.

When I was ten years old and living in a small town in southwest Missouri, I joined the Little League baseball team coached by my best friend's father. Three of my friends played on the team, and when we weren't at regular practices, we played baseball in an open field next to my best friend's house.

It was the happiest time of my life. I was "in the moment" hour after hour, day after day. All I wanted to do was catch, throw and hit a baseball. My pals would pitch to me and I would try to hit the ball harder, higher and further than before.

I don't remember the details of every practice and game, but I remember the thrill of hitting a home run. There were no fences on the playing field where we competed, so a home run was always an "inside-the-park" home run, where the runner had to hit the ball far enough so that he could speed around the bases before the throw reached home plate. I led the league that year with six home runs and was selected for the all-star team.

I also remember the time I was thrown out at third base. I felt as if I had let myself and my team down. As I walked toward my coach and teammates, I was so disappointed my eyes began to fill with tears. My coach put his arm around my shoulders and said, "I love it that you tried for the extra base. You always give it your all."

My father was in the service, and a year later when he was reassigned I had to leave my buddies behind. Unfortunately, in our new community there was no youth baseball program. But I found an outdoor basketball court, where I spent most of that summer immersed in the joy of repeatedly throwing a ball into a hoop. I developed a pretty consistent outside shot and had plenty of enthusiasm, so I played on the middle school basketball team.

By the time I was a freshman in high school, my father was reassigned to Germany, and we moved away again. At my new school, I discovered I was too small to compete on the high school team. So I fell in love with golf. Whenever the ground was clear of snow, I was on the course, often playing 36 holes a day. As a senior, I was captain of the golf team.

Later, at West Point I was required to take a physical fitness course and compete in intramural sports every semester. My favorite sports were wrestling and soccer.

Unlike many of my friends, I was never a varsity athlete. But sports definitely helped me ingrain life habits that prepared me for the challenges I would face in life.

Thanks to Title IX, young women now have abundant opportunities to participate in competitive team sports. In the Texas town where I live now, the local high school girls' tennis team recently won its seventh straight state championship. Can you imagine how all that work, competition and ultimate success has impacted the lives of these young student-athletes?

Associations, academies and schools across the nation are creating ever-expanding opportunities for young people to participate in every conceivable sport—all in the name of youth development.

It's a wonderful thing.

During the evolution of **Strong for Life**, our personal development system for teens, and **Strong for Mentoring Athletes**, our program for coaches, I studied what youth sports organizations are doing on national, regional and local levels. I learned that almost all these organizations publicly declare that their primary mission and purpose is youth development. Also, most of them are doing a good job helping volunteer coaches learn the sport and how to teach it to kids.

But I also discovered that in spite of all the good these organizations do, there's a huge opportunity to do more. Only a few of the hundreds of youth sports organizations recognize that most volunteer coaches need to improve the way they interact with youth. Like the adults in my learning and development programs, coaches have ingrained ways of dealing with others that can cause issues. To become effective mentors and achieve the sacred purpose of youth sports, most of them need to improve their coach-athlete communication skills.

As a result, not every team makes youth development its first priority. Not every coach is good with kids. Not every player has a positive growth experience, and not every kid is excited about coming back next year.

In the pages that follow, I will outline the key insights:

- Other adults besides parents are needed to raise a child to be a happy, responsible, successful adult.
- Youth sports are an important part of this "village."
- Most youth sports organizations acknowledge this purpose and make it their top priority.
- Youth sports really can help build the character strengths that prepare young people for life.
- The difference-maker is the coach.
- Coaches can become more effective mentors if they improve the way they communicate with young athletes.
- A few communication skills make a huge difference.
- Like learning to coach the game, improving coach-athlete communication skills requires a concerted effort over time.
- Youth sports organizations can magnify their impact on kids by addressing this shortfall.

"It takes a village to raise a child."

—*African proverb*

In his classic parenting books, *The Wonder of Boys* and *The Wonder of Girls*, psychologist Michael Gurian claims that "three families—not one" are needed to raise a healthy child to be a happy, successful adult.

The first family is the "nuclear family"—the parents and grandparents who raise the child.

The second family is the "extended family"—teachers, coaches, relatives, caretakers and other adult mentors.

The third family is the surrounding culture and community—media, churches, government and other institutions.

Gurian makes the case that raising a child to be a strong adult takes so much effort that a mother and father simply can't do it all. Both parents may be working; modern life is more complex than it used to be; and at a time when kids need guidance the most, they're spending more time away from home than with their parents.

Parents of ancient cultures traditionally relied on other adults to help guide a child through adolescence. But, the "tribe" or "village" is no longer a typical part of modern culture. In our mobile society, grown children often move away to create lives far from where they grew up. They may move many times, and their own children may be growing up in a community of strangers.

Furthermore, many nuclear families these days are headed by single parents. This is especially tricky when the single parent is trying to raise a child of the opposite sex. Moms have never been boys, and dads have never been girls, so they may not fully understand what their child needs.

In the best case, parents instinctively try to create a modern-day version of the village: relatives, teachers, athletic coaches, ministers and leaders in youth programs who will have a positive impact on their children.

---❖---

"Raw, ancient content is surging through youths' psyches, but adult culture over the last few centuries has forgotten how to meet, guide, and be replenished by its force."

– Michael Ventura
Author, *We've Had a Hundred Years of Therapy and the World Is Getting Worse*

"Most adolescent problems could be prevented if we brought back a unified, community-based approach to helping teens through this great developmental period of life."

– Bret Stephenson
Author, *From Boys to Men*

---❖---

Youth sports are an important part of the village.

I've described the positive influence sports had on my youth. Over the years, I've witnessed this same impact in the lives of hundreds of young people.

When my wife and I moved to the Texas Hill Country, our neighbor's daughter was in the fifth grade. Her parents, both retired from careers in the Air Force, were raising her with good values. The young lady soon became our go-to cat sitter.

She practiced volleyball relentlessly and eventually made the high school team. We watched her compete; she always gave a 100% effort. Later, she became a skilled horseback rider. Her dad introduced her to outdoor sports. He taught her how to fish and how to hunt with a bow and arrow. They went on father-daughter trips to Alaska to catch salmon and to Canada to hunt bear.

Now she's in college preparing for a career in wildlife management, and we're looking for a replacement cat-sitter. While her parents are visibly proud of her, they say it wasn't always smooth sailing. Without a doubt, her participation in youth sports was a major factor in her becoming the self-confident, action-oriented young woman she is now—someone who will become a productive contributor to society.

The avowed mission of youth sports organizations is "youth development"—to help young people grow stronger for life, through participation in sports.

Here are a few sample mission statements typical of those of hundreds of youth sports organizations.

The First Tee

...to impact the lives of young people by providing educational programs that build character, instill life-enhancing values and promote healthy choices through the game of golf.

Positive Coaching Alliance

...to develop "Better Athletes, Better People" by working to provide all youth and high school athletes a positive, character-building youth sports experience.

American Youth Soccer Organization

...to develop and deliver quality youth soccer programs which promote a fun, family environment based on AYSO's Six Philosophies: Everyone Plays®, Balanced Teams, Open Registration, Positive Coaching, Good Sportsmanship and Player Development.

Teach Grow Achieve (TGA)

...to introduce America's youth of all backgrounds to the fun, positive, character-building aspects of golf and tennis through programs that build life values, instill confidence through achievement, and offer a fun and educational experience.

Hockey Canada

...Lead, develop and promote

- *The values of fair play and sportsmanship, including the development of respect for all people by all participants.*
- *Hockey opportunities for all people regardless of age, gender, colour, race, ethnic origin, religion, sexual orientation, or socio-economic status and in both official languages.*
- *The importance for participants to develop dignity and self- esteem.*
- *The values of honesty and integrity in participants at all times.*
- *Teamwork, and the belief that what groups and society can achieve as a whole is greater than that which can be achieved by individuals.*
- *Canada's tradition in the game of hockey, and the proud and successful representation of this tradition around the world.*
- *The value of hard work, determination, the pursuit of excellence and success in all activities.*
- *The benefits of personal and physical well-being.*

It's often assumed that participation in a team sport will develop the kind of character strength that will help a child grow up to be a happy, responsible, successful adult.

The potential is certainly there, because a team sport is a microcosm of adult life, where success comes from acquiring specialized knowledge and skills, dealing with difficult challenges, striving against adversity, and working well with others to achieve individual and team goals.

Like sharpening an ax against a grindstone, young athletes can become stronger as individuals by dealing with the sport's inherent challenges. For example:

- It isn't easy to add a sport to an already busy schedule and show up for practice.
- It isn't easy to work on physical conditioning.
- It isn't easy to learn and follow the rules of a game.
- It isn't easy to acquire and refine new skills, and every sport involves numerous skills that take effort over time to master.
- It isn't easy to get along with a variety of different teammates.
- It isn't easy to accept a coach's corrections.
- It isn't easy to compete against other teams.
- It isn't easy to play a role while functioning as a team.

- It isn't easy to put a mistake behind you during the flow of a game.
- It isn't easy to keep trying when the other team is ahead.
- It isn't easy to keep your cool and stay focused when the contest gets physical.
- It isn't easy to give a total effort when you're tired.
- It isn't easy to exercise sportsmanship and grace in defeat.
- It isn't easy to work hard to get better during a long season.
- It isn't easy to rehab from an injury.

My study of youth sports and character development has taught me that participation can help a young person build a number of specific personal strengths: composure, cooperation, commitment, compassion, effort, excellence, initiative, integrity, perseverance, responsibility, self-confidence and self-discipline. These are the kinds of strengths that will not only help young people succeed in school, but are essential to building strong relationships and achieving goals later in a career.

But the potential benefits of participation in sports don't just happen. While most young people do grow from the experience, many don't. For them, participation can result in boredom, frustration, discouragement, disappointment, regret, or even an erosion of self-confidence and self-esteem.

The biggest difference-maker is the coach.

Many people in a youth sports organization play key roles, but it's the coach on the playing field who interacts with the young people and makes things happen.

Many volunteer coaches bring extensive experience to a program. Some of them have been elite athletes or have coached at a high level, and the kids can learn a lot from them about the game and related skills.

But will the coach put a high priority on youth development? Does the coach look for the character-building opportunities that come up in virtually every practice and competition? Does the coach know how to interact with the kids to translate these experiences into life lessons?

What I've learned from working with adults all these years is that very few of them have good communication skills. They're not very good listeners. They don't know the best way to give feedback, whether positive or negative. And they don't know how to coach someone to turn an experience into a life lesson.

In typical interactions with kids, emotions can take over. Minds close and discussions disintegrate into arguments and making demands. When kids don't do what's expected of them, sometimes adults respond with impatience, frustration, anger and other negative emotions; criticism and sarcasm; blame and shame; put-downs and name-calling.

But even though it's not uncommon for adults to fall back on ineffective, sometimes hurtful ways of communicating, my experience has taught me something important: *It's not their fault.*

When we adults were growing up and learning how to deal with each other, we weren't taught effective communication skills. While these are probably the most important skills a person can learn, they've never been a part of anyone's formal education. The assumption has always been that people learn how to interact through normal socialization. The idea has never caught on that there are effective ways to communicate and that there are quite a few interpersonal skills that can help people interact well with each other.

So when good-hearted volunteer coaches fail to turn sports participation into character-building experiences, it's not their fault that they don't know what to do differently.

These are some of the communication skills that are crucial for coaching athletes:

- Listening
- Giving feedback
- Giving encouragement
- Guiding learning

The reality is that very few coaches know the best way to use these skills. I've never met an adult who was good at all of them. The explanations and illustrations that follow make it clear how important they are.

---❖---

"Our chief want is someone who will inspire us to be what we know we could be."

– Ralph Waldo Emerson
American philosopher (1808-1882)

---❖---

Listening

A coach who doesn't engage with players will have little hope of transforming a player's participation into a personal development experience.

And this starts with being a good listener. When someone is trying to tell you something, the ultimate outcome is for both you and the speaker to feel sure that you actually understand the message.

Listening is different from conversation, and to engage the skill you need to know that it's time to do so. Most people don't realize when a "listening moment" is happening. They might be doing something else at the time and not give the speaker full attention. Or they might do more talking than listening in order to share their own stories and opinions. They might even interrupt the speaker to get their own points across.

The core skill of effective listening is to check what you think you've understood.

Listening is considered the most important communication skill because if the intended message isn't received, communication breaks down. Also, it's a component of several other communication skills. But few people are good listeners.

When coaches don't listen well, they can misunderstand their players, and kids can get the feeling that they haven't been heard. During adolescence, most young people are seeking greater independence, pushing away from their families and other adults. When they try to connect with an adult and it doesn't work, most kids stop trying.

Not so good...

Jackie: "Coach, I'm sorry I haven't been at practice."

Coach: "Well, it's like I told you before. You don't come to practice, you don't play."

Better...

Jackie: "Coach, I'm sorry I haven't been at practice."

Coach: "You have too much going on, more important things?"

Jackie: "No, my mom has to drive me and she's had to work late on a big project."

Coach: "I see."

Giving Constructive Feedback

It isn't easy to give effective feedback. It involves confronting an individual with the fact that their behavior is ineffective or unacceptable. Even adults who need feedback to be successful, who ask for it and welcome it—even pay for it—often feel uncomfortable receiving it.

Coaching athletes is all about pointing out shortcomings in order to help kids do things more effectively. So how should a coach do this without hurting a young person's feelings?

The answer is to focus on the behavior, not the athlete—to describe specifically what the young person is doing wrong, along with the consequences of that behavior. This should be followed by a specific description of the desired actions, and an expression of confidence that the athlete can achieve it. There are refinements to this technique that will avoid embarrassment in front of teammates.

Giving praise is similar—and easier. General statements such as "Attagirl," "Super," and "Good job" may feel good but they don't affirm what was done well. The best praise describes specifically what the child did right, followed by a sincere expression of delight.

Some coaches feel that criticism and put-downs are appropriate in sports because they help "toughen up" a kid for the rigors of competition. This is a misguided notion. Maybe some kids can handle it, especially if they're older. But the "tough love" approach can discourage a child, even erode self-confidence.

Not so good...

"Hey, Chris, what do you think you're doing out there?"

"Okay, I'm going to show you this again. This time, pay attention."

"Come on, Sally, get your act together."

"Good job, Bryce, you da man."

Better...

"You're not making good contact because you're swinging with your arms. That's why the ball gets by you before you can bring the bat around. Try it again, only this time, whip your body around while snapping your wrists."

"You missed it because you were out of position. You tried to go where the ball was, but by the time you got there it was somewhere else. The trick is to sense where the ball is headed and get there before the ball does."

"Sal, you did that exactly right. As you scooped up the ball, you pivoted on your left foot so you're facing first base when you throw. Perfect. I want to see you do that again."

Giving Encouragement

In sports, kids get discouraged. They make mistakes. They try to do well, but in the excitement of competition, they come up short. There are always winners and losers, and it doesn't feel good to lose.

The problem with discouragement is that if young people don't bounce back, they can give up on trying to improve. When kids lose heart, they don't enjoy themselves.

The best coaches have a knack for encouraging their players. Instead of denying what has happened and how the kids are reacting to it, they acknowledge it. They express empathy and understanding.

When discouraged, kids naturally focus on mistakes, failures and other negatives. A resilient child may be able to recover quickly from disappointment without encouragement, but most kids need a boost to avoid doubting themselves and giving up.

The best coaches, while acknowledging the negatives, help the kids see the positives in their situation. They also help the kids focus on the positives in themselves. Good encouragement reminds a player that yes, people made mistakes and things didn't go as planned. But good things happened, too. And even better things are possible in the future.

Not so good...

"You can do better than that."

"Get up, Jones. When you get knocked down, don't just feel sorry for yourself. Get back in it!"

"OK, you're tired, so what? Don't be a wuss."

Better...

"OK, you made a mistake and he took advantage of you. It happens. Nobody's perfect. There's a lot of time left, and I'm counting on you to put it behind you, focus on the next play."

"I know you feel embarrassed, but you've got a lot of talent and you're going to get better. It's early in the season. We'll work on that some more tomorrow, OK?"

"I know you're frustrated because you're not connecting with your backhand. It's a hard shot to learn. It takes a lot of practice. You just need to stick with it and get your reps in, and eventually it won't feel so awkward."

Guiding Learning

When it comes to teaching technique, a good approach is instruction, followed by demonstration, then lots of practice and coaching.

However, this approach doesn't work when teaching life lessons.

When most adults spot a learning opportunity, their instinct is to lecture, to make sure the lesson is made clear.

The problem is that young people don't react well to lectures. Even if they know the adult is right, they don't like being preached to. It's too much like a put-down. They may endure the lecture in silence, but they discount what they're being told.

A better method is to ask open-ended questions that guide the youth to discover the lesson.

"What happened out there?"

"Why do you think it happened that way?"

"What were the consequences?"

"What's a better way to handle that situation?"

Most coaches aren't familiar with this way of guiding learning; but when it comes to helping kids build character strength through sports, it's many times more effective than a lecture.

❖

"Too often we underestimate the power of a touch, a smile, a kind word, a listening ear, an honest compliment, or the smallest act of caring, all of which have the potential to turn a life around."

– Leo Buscaglia
American author (1924-1998)

"Feedback is the breakfast of champions."

– Ken Blanchard
American author (1939-)

❖

My research confirmed that most youth sports organizations are doing a good job of preparing coaches to teach the game; and as online technology advances, they're getting better at this all the time. Some programs have created excellent multi-level coach certification courses.

> **But for youth sports to achieve its purpose, coaches need to improve the way they interact with kids.**

This is crucial to using what happens on the field to create life lessons.

The coaches themselves typically aren't conscious of issues about the way they communicate with kids. Even if they were, they wouldn't know what to do about it. They may not appreciate that improving only a few specific skills can make a world of difference.

And when it comes to the kids, most coaches don't know which specific aspects of character can actually grow stronger through sports—or how to facilitate this kind of learning. They don't realize that character strengths are actually behavior patterns like other skills, which can be reinforced through coaching.

For youth sports organizations that profess to make youth development their top priority, this is a huge problem. In my assessment, it's *the* problem.

It's also a huge opportunity for the leaders of youth programs, because coach-athlete communication skills can be improved.

> This is the promising future of youth sports: to empower coaches to be more effective mentors to their athletes—more confident, skilled facilitators of youth development.

Achieving this will help youth sports programs fulfill their sacred purpose of youth development, producing significant benefits for everyone involved:

- More kids' lives positively impacted
- More kids attracted to the sport
- More parents happy with the coaches
- More parents giving support to the program
- More adults volunteering to be coaches
- More athletes returning to participate the following year

To be fair, the sport itself—not how coaches communicate—is the primary area of expertise of youth sports organizations. But if these programs are to achieve their purpose of helping kids grow stronger for life, they'll need to integrate coach development programs that focus on coach-athlete communication skills.

My work has taught me what it takes to change an adult's behavior. Administrators of youth sports programs need to appreciate that it takes a lot more than the right mission statement or a carefully worded policy letter. To replace problem ways of reacting with effective ones takes more than a video or two.

The reason is that on the field, coaches react. They don't consciously decide how they'll talk to an athlete. Changing coaches' behavior patterns will take a long-term program of enlightenment, reinforcement, feedback and encouragement.

In other words, volunteer coaches will need to "do the reps." They'll need to grow stronger along with their athletes.

To address this crying need, I've developed **Strong for Mentoring Athletes**, an online brain-based learning system for improving coach-athlete communication skills and the character strengths coaches need to model.

The system directs coaches to focus on one behavior pattern at a time and guides them to apply the program's content during real-world practices and competition. Afterwards, they return to the program to record what they learned from the experience. They repeat this cycle of focus, action and reflection until the skill or strength feels natural and automatic.

Administrators of the system can easily customize the look of the program and add their own sport-related content, effectively integrating this aspect of coach development with other training materials. While the coaches' personal learning entries are confidential, administrators have access to a dashboard to monitor usage and communicate with the coaches.

There's much more to this innovative learning resource than I can describe here. To learn more and request an online demo, visit:

www.StrongForMentoringAthletes.com

About the Author

Dr. Dennis Coates has been CEO of Performance Systems, Inc., since 1987. For more than 25 years his passionate interest in the human brain—how it develops, learns and makes decisions—has informed his learning innovations. In 1994 he created **20/20 Insight**, a multi-source performance feedback system that has been used by millions of people worldwide. In 2010 he developed **ProStar Coach**, an online virtual coaching service for developing the communication skills and personal strengths people need to meet the challenges of work and life.

Today, his original focus on adult learning and development has expanded to parenting and youth development. The **ProStar Coach** platform serves a family of learning systems aimed at the "village" of adult mentors, to improve their ability to help young people grow up to be responsible, happy, successful adults:

- **Strong for Mentoring Athletes** (for coaches)
- **Strong for Parenting** (for parents)
- **Strong for Mentoring Students** (for teachers)
- **Strong for Mentoring Youth** (for youth program leaders)
- **Strong for Life** (for young people)